CW00730808

CONTENTS

LINES INSCRIBED UPON A CUP
FORMED FROM A SKULL

Start not – nor deem my spirit fled;
   In me behold the only skull,
From which, unlike a living head,
   Whatever flows is never dull.

I lived, I loved, I quaff'd, like thee:
   I died: let earth my bones resign;
Fill up – thou canst not injure me;
   The worm hath fouler lips than thine.

Better to hold the sparkling grape,
   Than nurse the earth-worm's slimy brood;
And circle in the goblet's shape
   The drink of gods, than reptile's food.

Where once my wit, perchance, hath shone,
   In aid of others' let me shine;
And when, alas! our brains are gone,
   What nobler substitute than wine?

Quaff while thou canst: another race,
   When thou and thine, like me, are sped,
May rescue thee from earth's embrace,
   And rhyme and revel with the dead.

Why not? since through life's little day
   Our heads such sad effects produce;
Redeem'd from worms and wasting clay,
   This chance is theirs, to be of use.

WHEN WE TWO PARTED

When we two parted
    In silence and tears,
Half broken-hearted
    To sever for years,
Pale grew thy cheek and cold,
    Colder thy kiss;
Truly that hour foretold
    Sorrow to this.

The dew of the morning
    Sunk chill on my brow –
It felt like the warning
    Of what I feel now.
Thy vows are all broken,
    And light is thy fame;
I hear thy name spoken,
    And share in its shame.

They name thee before me,
    A knell to mine ear;
A shudder comes o'er me –
    Why wert thou so dear?
They know not I knew thee,
    Who knew thee too well: –
Long, long shall I rue thee,
    Too deeply to tell.

In secret we met –
   In silence I grieve,
That thy heart could forget,
   Thy spirit deceive.
If I should meet thee
   After long years,
How should I greet thee? –
   With silence and tears.

STANZAS TO AUGUSTA

Though the day of my destiny's over,
   And the star of my fate hath declined,
Thy soft heart refused to discover
   The faults which so many could find;
Though thy soul with my grief was acquainted,
   It shrunk not to share it with me,
And the love which my spirit hath painted
   It never hath found but in *thee*.

Then when nature around me is smiling,
   The last smile which answers to mine,
I do not believe it beguiling,
   Because it reminds me of thine;
And when winds are at war with the ocean,
   As the breasts I believed in with me,
If their billows excite an emotion,
   It is that they bear me from *thee*.

Though the rock of my last hope is shivered,
   And its fragments are sunk in the wave,
Though I feel that my soul is delivered
   To pain – it shall not be its slave.
There is many a pang to pursue me:
   They may crush, but they shall not contemn;
They may torture, but shall not subdue me –
   'Tis of *thee* that I think – not of them.

Though human, thou didst not deceive me,
   Though woman, thou didst not forsake,
Though loved, thou forborest to grieve me,
   Though slandered, thou never couldst shake;
Though trusted, thou didst not disclaim me,
   Though parted, it was not to fly,
Though watchful, 'twas not to defame me,
   Nor, mute, that the world might belie.

Yet I blame not the world, nor despise it,
  Nor the war of the many with one;
If my soul was not fitted to prize it,
  'Twas folly not sooner to shun:
And if dearly that error hath cost me,
  And more than I once could foresee,
I have found that, whatever it lost me,
  It could not deprive me of *thee*.

From the wreck of the past, which hath perished,
  Thus much I at least may recall,
It hath taught me that what I most cherished
  Deserved to be dearest of all:
In the desert a fountain is springing,
  In the wide waste there still is a tree,
And a bird in the solitude singing,
  Which speaks to my spirit of *thee*.

THE DESTRUCTION OF SENNACHERIB

The Assyrian came down like the wolf on the fold,
And his cohorts were gleaming in purple and gold;
And the sheen of their spears was like stars on the sea,
When the blue wave rolls nightly on deep Galilee.

Like the leaves of the forest when summer is green,
That host with their banners at sunset were seen;
Like the leaves of the forest when autumn hath blown,
That host on the morrow lay withered and strown.

For the Angel of Death spread his wings on the blast,
And breathed in the face of the foe as he passed;
And the eyes of the sleepers waxed deadly and chill,
And their hearts but once heaved, and for ever grew
  still!

And there lay the steed with his nostril all wide,
But through it there rolled not the breath of his pride;
And the foam of his gasping lay white on the turf,
And cold as the spray of the rock-beating surf.

And there lay the rider distorted and pale,
With the dew on his brow, and the rust on his mail:
And the tents were all silent, the banners alone,
The lances unlifted, the trumpet unblown.

And the widows of Ashur are loud in their wail,
And the idols are broke in the temple of Baal;
And the might of the Gentile, unsmote by the sword,
Hath melted like snow in the glance of the Lord!

FARE THEE WELL

Fare thee well! and if for ever,
    Still for ever, fare thee well:
Even though unforgiving, never
    'Gainst thee shall my heart rebel.

Would that breast were bared before thee
    Where thy head so oft hath lain,
While that placid sleep came o'er thee
    Which thou ne'er canst know again:

Would that breast, by thee glanced over,
    Every inmost thought could show!
Then thou wouldst at last discover
    'Twas not well to spurn it so.

Though the world for this commend thee –
    Though it smile upon the blow,
Even its praises must offend thee,
    Founded on another's woe:

Though my many faults defaced me,
    Could no other arm be found,
Than the one which once embraced me,
    To inflict a cureless wound?

Yet, oh yet, thyself deceive not;
　　Love may sink by slow decay,
But by sudden wrench, believe not
　　Hearts can thus be torn away:

Still thine own its life retaineth –
　　Still must mine, though bleeding, beat;
And the undying thought which paineth
　　Is – that we no more may meet.

These are words of deeper sorrow
　　Than the wail above the dead;
Both shall live, but every morrow
　　Wake us from a widowed bed.

And when thou would solace gather,
　　When our child's first accents flow,
Wilt thou teach her to say 'Father!'
　　Though his care she must forego?

When her little hands shall press thee,
　　When her lip to thine is pressed,
Think of him whose prayer shall bless thee,
　　Think of him thy love *had* blessed!

Should her lineaments resemble
  Those thou never more may'st see,
Then thy heart will softly tremble
  With a pulse yet true to me. .

All my faults perchance thou knowest,
  All my madness none can know;
All my hopes, where'er thou goest,
  Wither, yet with *thee* they go.

Every feeling hath been shaken;
  Pride, which not a world could bow,
Bows to thee – by thee forsaken,
  Even my soul forsakes me now:

But 'tis done – all words are idle –
  Words from me are vainer still;
But the thoughts we cannot bridle
  Force their way without the will.

Fare thee well! thus disunited,
  Torn from every nearer tie,
Seared in heart, and lone, and blighted,
  More than this I scarce can die.

SHE WALKS IN BEAUTY

She walks in beauty, like the night
   Of cloudless climes and starry skies;
And all that's best of dark and bright
   Meet in her aspect and her eyes:
Thus mellowed to that tender light
   Which heaven to gaudy day denies.

One shade the more, one ray the less,
   Had half impaired the nameless grace,
Which waves in every raven tress,
   Or softly lightens o'er her face;
Where thoughts serenely sweet express,
   How pure, how dear their dwelling-place.

And on that cheek, and o'er that brow,
   So soft, so calm, yet eloquent,
The smiles that win, the tints that glow,
   But tell of days in goodness spent,
A mind at peace with all below,
   A heart whose love is innocent!

TO THOMAS MOORE

My boat is on the shore,
   And my bark is on the sea;
But, before I go, Tom Moore,
   Here's a double health to thee!

Here's a sigh to those who love me,
   And a smile to those who hate;
And, whatever sky's above me,
   Here's a heart for every fate.

Though the ocean roar around me,
   Yet it still shall bear me on;
Though a desert should surround me,
   It hath springs that may be won.

Were't the last drop in the well,
   As I gasped upon the brink,
Ere my fainting spirit fell,
   'Tis to thee that I would drink.

With that water, as this wine,
   The libation I would pour
Should be – peace with thine and mine,
   And a health to thee, Tom Moore.

JOHN KEATS

Who killed John Keats?
  'I,' says the Quarterly,
So savage and Tartarly;
  'Twas one of my feats.'

Who shot the arrow?
  'The poet-priest Milman
(So ready to kill man),
  Or Southey or Barrow.'

ONE STRUGGLE MORE, AND I AM FREE

One struggle more, and I am free
    From pangs that rend my heart in twain;
One last long sigh to love and thee,
    Then back to busy life again.
It suits me well to mingle now
    With things that never pleased before:
Though every joy is fled below,
    What future grief can touch me more?

Then bring me wine, the banquet bring;
    Man was not formed to live alone:
I'll be that light, unmeaning thing,
    That smiles with all, and weeps with none.
It was not thus in days more dear,
    It never would have been, but thou
Hast fled, and left me lonely here;
    Thou'rt nothing, – all are nothing now.

In vain my lyre would lightly breathe!
　　The smile that sorrow fain would wear
But mocks the woe that lurks beneath,
　　Like roses o'er a sepulchre.
Though gay companions o'er the bowl
　　Dispel awhile the sense of ill;
Though pleasure fires the maddening soul,
　　The heart – the heart is lonely still!

On many a lone and lovely night
　　It soothed to gaze upon the sky;
For then I deemed the heavenly light
　　Shone sweetly on thy pensive eye:
And oft I thought at Cynthia's noon,
　　When sailing o'er the Aegean wave,
'Now Thyrza gazes on that moon' –
　　Alas, it gleamed upon her grave!

When stretched on fever's sleepless bed,
    And sickness shrunk my throbbing veins.
''Tis comfort still,' I faintly said,
    'That Thyrza cannot know my pains:'
Like freedom to the time-worn slave –
    A boon 'tis idle then to give –
Relenting Nature vainly gave
    My life, when Thyrza ceased to live!

My Thyrza's pledge in better days,
    When love and life alike were new!
How different now thou meet'st my gaze!
    How tinged by time with sorrow's hue!
The heart that gave itself with thee
    Is silent – ah, were mine as still!
Though cold as e'en the dead can be,
    It feels, it sickens with the chill.

Thou bitter pledge! thou mournful token!
   Though painful, welcome to my breast!
Still, still, preserve that love unbroken,
   Or break the heart to which thou'rt pressed!
Time tempers love, but not removes,
   More hallowed when its hope is fled:
Oh! what are thousand living loves
   To that which cannot quit the dead?

AND THOU ART DEAD, AS YOUNG AND FAIR

'Heu, quanto minus est cum
reliquis versari quam tui meminisse!'

And thou art dead, as young and fair,
   As aught of mortal birth;
And form so soft, and charms so rare,
   Too soon returned to Earth!
Though Earth received them in her bed,
And o'er the spot the crowd may tread
   In carelessness or mirth,
There is an eye which could not brook
A moment on that grave to look.

I will not ask where thou liest low,
   Nor gaze upon the spot;
There flowers or weeds at will may grow,
   So I behold them not:
It is enough for me to prove
That what I loved, and long must love,
   Like common earth can rot;
To me there needs no stone to tell,
'Tis Nothing that I loved so well.

Yet did I love thee to the last
    As fervently as thou,
Who didst not change through all the past,
    And canst not alter now.
The love where Death has set his seal,
Nor age can chill, nor rival steal,
    Nor falsehood disavow:
And, what were worse, thou canst not see
Or wrong, or change, or fault in me.

The better days of life were ours;
    The worst can be but mine:
The sun that cheers, the storm that lowers,
    Shall never more be thine.
The silence of that dreamless sleep
I envy now too much to weep;
    Nor need I to repine
That all those charms have passed away;
I might have watched through long decay.

The flower in ripened bloom unmatched
    Must fall the earliest prey;
Though by no hand untimely snatched,
    The leaves must drop away:
And yet it were a greater grief
To watch it withering, leaf by leaf,
    Than see it plucked today;
Since earthly eye but ill can bear
To trace the change to foul from fair.

I know not if I could have borne
    To see thy beauties fade;
The night that followed such a morn
    Had worn a deeper shade:
Thy day without a cloud hath passed,
And thou wert lovely to the last;
    Extinguished, not decayed;
As stars that shoot along the sky
Shine brightest as they fall from high.

As once I wept, if I could weep,
  My tears might well be shed,
To think I was not near to keep
  One vigil o'er thy bed;
To gaze, how fondly! on thy face,
To fold thee in a faint embrace,
  Uphold thy drooping head;
And show that love, however vain,
Nor thou nor I can feel again.

Yet how much less it were to gain,
  Though thou hast left me free,
The loveliest things that still remain,
  Than thus remember thee!
The all of thine that cannot die
Through dark and dread Eternity
  Returns again to me,
And more thy buried love endears
Than aught, except its living years.

STANZAS FOR MUSIC - 1

There's not a joy the world can give like that it takes
    away.
When the glow of early thought declines in feeling's
    dull decay;
'Tis not on youth's smooth cheek the blush alone,
    which fades so fast,
But the tender bloom of heart is gone, ere youth itself
    be past.

Then the few whose spirits float above the wreck of
    happiness
Are driven o'er the shoals of guilt or ocean of excess:
The magnet of their course is gone, or only points in
    vain
The shore to which their shivered sail shall never
    stretch again.

Then the mortal coldness of the soul like death itself
comes down.
It cannot feel for others' woes, it dare not dream its
own;
That heavy chill has frozen o'er the fountain of our
tears,
And though the eye may sparkle still, 'tis where the
ice appears.

Though wit may flash from fluent lips, and mirth
distract the breast,
Through midnight hours that yield no more their
former hope of rest;
'Tis but as ivy-leaves around the ruined turret wreath,
All green and wildly fresh without, but worn and grey
beneath.

Oh could I feel as I have felt, - or be what I have
been,
Or weep as I could once have wept, o'er many a
vanished scene;
As springs in deserts found seem sweet, all brackish
though they be,
So midst the withered waste of life, those tears would
flow to me.

There be none of beauty's daughters
   With a magic like thee;
And like music on the waters
   Is thy sweet voice to me:
When, as if its sound were causing
The charméd ocean's pausing,
The waves lie still and gleaming,
And the lulled winds seem dreaming:

And the midnight moon is weaving
   Her bright chain o'er the deep;
Whose breast is gently heaving,
   As an infant's asleep:
So the spirit bows before thee,
To listen and adore thee;
With a full but soft emotion,
Like the swell of summer's ocean.

From ENGLISH BARDS AND SCOTCH REVIEWERS

Time was, ere yet in these degenerate days
Ignoble themes obtained mistaken praise,
When sense and wit with poesy allied,
No fabled graces, flourished side by side;
From the same fount their inspiration drew,
And, reared by taste, bloomed fairer as they grew.
Then, in this happy isle, a Pope's pure strain
Sought the rapt soul to charm, nor sought in vain;
A polished nation's praise aspired to claim,
And raised the people's, as the poet's fame.
Like him great Dryden poured the tide of song,
In stream less smooth, indeed, yet doubly strong.
Then Congreve's scenes could cheer, or Otway's melt;
For Nature then an English audience felt—
But why these names, or greater still, retrace,
When all to feebler bards resign their place?
Yet to such times our lingering looks are cast,
When taste and reason with those times are past.
Now look around, and turn each trifling page,
Survey the precious works that please the age;
This truth at least let satire's self allow,
No dearth of bards can be complained of now.
The loaded press beneath her labour groans,
And printer's devils shake their weary bones;
While Southey's epics cram the creaking shelves,
And Little's lyrics shine in hot-pressed twelves.
Thus saith the Preacher: 'Nought beneath the sun

Is new;' yet still from change to change we run.
What varied wonders tempt us as they pass!
The cow-pox, tractors, galvanism, and gas,
In turns appear, to make the vulgar stare,
Till the swoln bubble bursts – and all is air!
Nor less new schools of poetry arise,
Where dull pretenders grapple for the prize:
O'er taste awhile these pseudo-bards prevail;
Each country book-club bows the knee to Baal,
And, hurling lawful genius from the throne,
Erects a shrine and idol of its own;
Some leaden calf – but whom it matters not,
From soaring Southey, down to grovelling Stott.

*　　*　　*

Next comes the dull disciple of thy school,
That mild apostate from poetic rule,
The simple Wordsworth, framer of a lay
As soft as evening in his favourite May,
Who warns his friend 'to shake off toil and trouble,
And quit his books, for fear of growing double;'
Who, both by precept and example, shows
That prose is verse, and verse is merely prose;

Convincing all, by demonstration plain,
Poetic souls delight in prose insane;
And Christmas stories tortured into rhyme
Contain the essence of the true sublime.
Thus, when he tells the tale of Betty Foy,
The idiot mother of 'an idiot boy;'
A moon-struck, silly lad, who lost his way,
And, like his bard, confounded night with day;
So close on each pathetic part he dwells,
And each adventure so sublimely tells,
That all who view the 'idiot in his glory'
Conceive the Bard the hero of the story.

From THE GIAOUR

To love the softest hearts are prone,
But such can ne'er be all his own;
Too timid in his woes to share,
Too meek to meet, or brave despair;
And sterner hearts alone may feel
The wound that time can never heal.
The rugged metal of the mine,
Must burn before its surface shine,
But plunged within the furnace-flame,
It bends and melts – though still the same;
Then tempered to thy want, or will,
'Twill serve thee to defend or kill;
A breast-plate for thine hour of need,
Or blade to bid thy foeman bleed;
But if a dagger's form it bear,
Let those who shape its edge, beware!
Thus passion's fire, and woman's art,
Can turn and tame the sterner heart;
From these its form and tone are ta'en,
And what they make it, must remain,
But break – before it bend again.

*   *   *

If solitude succeed to grief,
Release from pain is slight relief;
The vacant bosom's wilderness
Might thank the pang that made it less.
We loathe what none are left to share:

Even bliss – 'twere woe alone to bear;
The heart once left thus desolate
Must fly at last for ease – to hate.
It is as if the dead could feel
The icy worm around them steal,
And shudder, as the reptiles creep
To revel o'er their rotting sleep,
Without the power to scare away
The cold consumers of their clay!
It is as if the desert-bird,
　　Whose beak unlocks her bosom's stream
　　To still her famished nestlings' scream,
Nor mourns a life to them transferred,
Should rend her rash devoted breast,
And find them flown her empty nest.
The keenest pangs the wretched find
　　Are rapture to the dreary void,
The leafless desert of the mind,
　　The waste of feelings unemployed.
Who would be doomed to gaze upon
A sky without a cloud or sun?
Less hideous far the tempest's roar
Than ne'er to brave the billows more –
Thrown, when the war of winds is o'er,
A lonely wreck on fortune's shore,
'Mid sullen calm, and silent bay,
Unseen to drop by dull decay; –
Better to sink beneath the shock
Than moulder piecemeal on the rock!

From THE VISION OF JUDGMENT

Saint Peter sat by the celestial gate:
   His keys were rusty, and the lock was dull,
So little trouble had been given of late;
   Not that the place by any means was full,
But since the Gallic era 'eighty-eight'
   The devils had ta'en a longer, stronger pull,
And 'a pull altogether', as they say
At sea – which drew most souls another way.

The angels all were singing out of tune,
   And hoarse with having little else to do,
Excepting to wind up the sun and moon,
   Or curb a runaway young star or two,
Or wild colt of a comet, which too soon
   Broke out of bounds o'er the ethereal blue,
Splitting some planet with its playful tail,
As boats are sometimes by a wanton whale.

The guardian seraphs had retired on high,
    Finding their charges past all care below:
Terrestrial business filled nought in the sky
    Save the recording angel's black bureau:
Who found, indeed, the facts to multiply
    With such rapidity of vice and woe,
That he had stripped off both his wings in quills,
And yet was in arrear of human ills.

His business so augmented of late years,
    That he was forced, against his will, no doubt,
(Just like those cherubs, earthly ministers,)
    For some resource to turn himself about,
And claim the help of his celestial peers,
    To aid him ere he should be quite worn out,
By the increased demand for his remarks:
Six angels and twelve saints were named his clerks.

This was a handsome board - at least for heaven;
    And yet they had even then enough to do,
So many conquerors' cars were daily driven,
    So many kingdoms fitted up anew;
Each day, too, slew its thousands six or seven,
    Till at the crowning carnage, Waterloo,
They threw their pens down in divine disgust -
The page was so besmeared with blood and dust.

CHILDE HAROLD'S PILGRIMAGE

From Canto 1

Oh, thou! in Hellas deemed of heavenly birth,
Muse! formed or fabled at the minstrel's will!
Since shamed full oft by later lyres on earth,
Mine dares not call thee from thy sacred hill:
Yet there I've wandered by thy vaunted rill;
Yes! sighed o'er Delphi's long deserted shrine,
Where, save that feeble fountain, all is still;
Nor mote my shell awake the weary Nine
To grace so plain a tale – this lowly lay of mine.

Whilome in Albion's isle there dwelt a youth,
Who ne in virtue's ways did take delight;
But spent his days in riot most uncouth,
And vexed with mirth the drowsy ear of night.
Ah, me! in sooth he was a shameless wight,
Sore given to revel and ungodly glee;
Few earthly things found favour in his sight
Save concubines and carnal companie,
And flaunting wassailers of high and low degree.

Childe Harold was he hight: – but whence his name
And lineage long, it suits me not say;
Suffice it, that perchance they were of fame,
And had been glorious in another day:
But one sad losel soils a name for aye,
However mighty in the olden time;
Nor all that heralds rake from coffined clay,
Nor florid prose, nor honied lies of rhyme,
Can blazon evil deeds, or consecrate a crime.

Childe Harolde basked him in the noontide sun,
Disporting there like any other fly;
Nor deemed before his little day was done
One blast might chill him into misery.
But long ere scarce a third of his passed by,
Worse than adversity the Childe befell;
He felt the fulness of satiety:
Then loathed he in his native land to dwell,
Which seemed to him more lone than Eremite's sad
cell.

For he through Sin's long labyrinth had run,
Nor made atonement when he did amiss,
Had sighed to many though he loved but one,
And that loved one, alas! could ne'er be his.
Ah, happy she! to 'scape from him whose kiss
Had been pollution unto aught so chaste;
Who soon had left her charms for vulgar bliss,
And spoiled her goodly lands to gild his waste,
Nor calm domestic peace had ever deigned to taste.

And now Childe Harold was sore sick at heart,
And from his fellow bacchanals would flee;
'Tis said, at times the sullen tear would start,
But pride congealed the drop within his ee:
Apart he stalked in joyless reverie,
And from his native land resolved to go,
And visit scorching climes beyond the sea;
With pleasure drugged, he almost longed for woe,
And e'en for change of scene would seek the shades
   below.

The Childe departed from his father's hall:
It was a vast and venerable pile;
So old, it seeméd only not to fall,
Yet strength was pillared in each massy aisle.
Monastic dome! condemned to uses vile!
Where superstition once had made her den
Now Paphian girls were known to sing and smile;
And monks might deem their time was come agen,
If ancient tales say true, nor wrong these holy men.

Yet oft-times in his maddest mirthful mood
Strange pangs would flash along Childe Harold's
brow,
As if the memory of some deadly feud
Or disappointed passion lurked below:
But this none knew, nor haply cared to know;
For his was not that open, artless soul
That feels relief by bidding sorrow flow,
Nor sought he friend to counsel or condole,
Whate'er this grief mote be, which he could not
control.

And none did love him! – though to hall and bower
He gathered revellers from far and near,
He knew them flatterers of the festal hour;
The heartless parasites of present cheer.
Yea! none did love him – not his lemans dear –
But pomp and power alone are woman's care,
And where these are light Eros finds a feere;
Maidens, like moths, are ever caught by glare,
And Mammon wins his way where Seraphs might
despair.

Childe Harold had a mother – not forgot,
Though parting from that mother he did shun;
A sister whom he loved, but saw her not
Before his weary pilgrimage begun:
If friends he had, he bade adieu to none.
Yet deem not thence his breast a breast of steel:
Ye, who have known what 'tis to dote upon
A few dear objects, will in sadness feel
Such partings break the heart they fondly hope to
heal.

His house, his home, his heritage, his lands,
The laughing dames in whom he did delight,
Whose large blue eyes, fair locks, and snowy hands,
Might shake the saintship of an anchorite,
And long had fed his youthful appetite;
His goblets brimmed with every costly wine,
And all that mote to luxury invite,
Without a sigh, he left to cross the brine,
And traverse Paynim shores, and pass Earth's central
line.

The sails were filled, and fair the light winds blew,
As glad to waft him from his native home;
And fast the white rocks faded from his view,
And soon were lost in circumambient foam:
And then, it may be, of his wish to roam
Repented he, but in his bosom slept
The silent thought, nor from his lips did come
One word of wail, whilst others sate and wept,
And to the reckless gales unmanly moaning kept.

But when the sun was sinking in the sea
He seized his harp, which he at times could string,
And strike, albeit with untaught melody,
When deemed he no strange ear was listening:
And now his fingers o'er it he did fling,
And tuned his farewell in the dim twilight.
While flew the vessel on her snowy wing,
And fleeting shores receded from his sight,
Thus to the elements he poured his last 'Good Night'.

'Adieu, adieu! my native shore
  Fades o'er the waters blue;
The night-winds sigh, the breakers roar,
  And shrieks the wild sea-mew.
Yon sun that sets upon the sea
  We follow in his flight;
Farewell awhile to him and thee,
  My native land – Good Night!

CHILDE HAROLD'S PILGRIMAGE

From Canto 3

I have not loved the world, nor the world me;
I have not flattered its rank breath, nor bowed
To its idolatries a patient knee,
Nor coined my cheek to smiles, – nor cried aloud
In worship of an echo; in the crowd
They could not deem me one of such – I stood
Among them, but not of them – in a shroud
Of thoughts which were not their thoughts, and still
    could,
Had I not filed my mind, which thus itself subdued.

I have not loved the world, nor the world me, –
But let us part fair foes; I do believe,
Though I have found them not, that there may be
Words which are things, – hopes which will not
    deceive,
And virtues which are merciful, nor weave
Snares for the failing: I would also deem
O'er others' griefs that some sincerely grieve;
That two, or one, are almost what they seem, –
That goodness is no name, and happiness no
    dream. . . .

CHILDE HAROLD'S PILGRIMAGE

From Canto 4

The moon is up, and yet it is not night –
Sunset divides the sky with her – a sea
Of glory streams along the Alpine height
Of blue Friuli's mountains; Heaven is free
From clouds, but of all colours seems to be
Melted to one vast Iris of the west,
Where the day joins the past eternity;
While, on the other hand, meek Dian's crest
Floats through the azure air – an island of the blest!

A single star is at her side, and reigns
With her o'er half the lovely heaven; but still
Yon sunny sea heaves brightly, and remains
Rolled o'er the peak of the far Rhaetian hill,
As day and night contending were, until
Nature reclaimed her order: – gently flows
The deep-dyed Brenta, where their hues instil
The odorous purple of a new-born rose,
Which streams upon her stream, and glassed within it
glows,

Filled with the face of heaven, which, from afar,
Comes down upon the waters! all its hues,
From the rich sunset to the rising star,
Their magical variety diffuse:
And now they change – a paler shadow strews
Its mantle o'er the mountains; parting day
Dies like the dolphin, whom each pang imbues
With a new colour as it gasps away,
The last still loveliest, till – 'tis gone – and all is grey.

CHILDE HAROLD'S PILGRIMAGE

From Canto 4

I see before me the Gladiator lie:
He leans upon his hand – his manly brow
Consents to death, but conquers agony,
And his drooped head sinks gradually low –
And through his side the last drops, ebbing slow
From the red gash, fall heavy, one by one,
Like the first of a thunder-shower; and now
The arena swims around him – he is gone,
Ere ceased the inhuman shout which hailed the wretch
    who won.

He heard it, but he heeded not – his eyes
Were with his heart, and that was far away;
He recked not of the life he lost nor prize,
But where his rude hut by the Danube lay,
There were his young barbarians all at play,
There was their Dacian mother – he, their sire,
Butchered to make a Roman holiday –
All this rushed with his blood – Shall he expire
And unavenged? – Arise! ye Goths, and glut your ire!

But here, where murder breathed her bloody steam;
And here, where buzzing nations choked the ways,
And roared or murmured like a mountain stream
Dashing or winding as its torrent strays;
Here, where the Roman million's blame or praise
Was death or life, the playthings of a crowd;
My voice sounds much – and fall the stars' faint
     rays
On the arena void – seats crushed – walls bowed –
And galleries, where my steps seem echoes strangely
     loud.

A ruin – yet what ruin! from its mass
Walls, palaces, half-cities, have been reared;
Yet oft the enormous skeleton ye pass,
And marvel where the spoil could have appeared.
Hath it indeed been plundered, or but cleared?
Alas! developed, opens the decay,
When the colossal fabric's form is neared:
It will not bear the brightness of the day,
Which streams too much on all years, man, have reft
     away.

But when the rising moon begins to climb
Its topmost arch, and gently pauses there;
When the stars twinkle through the loops of time,
And the low night-breeze waves along the air
The garland-forest, which the grey walls wear,
Like laurels on the bald first Caesar's head;
When the light shines serene but doth not glare,
Then in this magic circle raise the dead:
Heroes have trod this spot – 'tis on their dust ye tread.

'While stands the Coliseum, Rome shall stand;
'When falls the Coliseum, Rome shall fall;
'And when Rome falls – the World.' From our own
land
Thus spake the pilgrims o'er this mighty wall
In Saxon times, which we are wont to call
Ancient; and these three mortal things are still
On their foundations, and unaltered all;
Rome and her ruin past redemption's skill,
The World, the same wide den – of thieves, or what
ye will. . . .

But I forget. – My Pilgrim's shrine is won,
And he and I must part – so let it be –
His task and mine alike are nearly done;
Yet once more let us look upon the sea;
The midland ocean breaks on him and me,
And from the Alban Mount we now behold
Our friend of youth, that ocean, which when we
Beheld it last by Calpe's rock unfold
Those waves, we followed on till the dark Euxine
    rolled

Upon the blue Symplegades; long years –
Long, though not very many, since have done
Their work on both; some suffering and some tears
Have left us nearly where we had begun:
Yet not in vain our mortal race hath run,
We have had our reward – and it is here;
That we can yet feel gladdened by the sun,
And reap from earth, sea, joy almost as dear
As if there were no man to trouble what is clear.

Oh! that the desert were my dwelling-place,
With one fair spirit for my minister,
That I might all forget the human race,
And, hating no one, love but only her!
Ye elements! – in whose ennobling stir
I feel myself exalted – can ye not
Accord me such a being? Do I err
In deeming such inhabit many a spot?
Though with them to converse can rarely be our lot.

There is a pleasure in the pathless woods,
There is a rapture on the lonely shore,
There is society, where none intrudes,
By the deep sea, and music in its roar:
I love not Man the less, but Nature more,
From these our interviews, in which I steal
From all I may be, or have been before,
To mingle with the universe, and feel
What I can ne'er express, yet can not all conceal.

Roll on, thou deep and dark blue ocean – roll!
Ten thousand fleets sweep over thee in vain;
Man marks the earth with ruin – his control
Stops with the shore; – upon the watery plain
The wrecks are all thy deed, nor doth remain
A shadow of man's ravage, save his own,
When, for a moment, like a drop of rain,
He sinks into thy depths with bubbling groan,
Without a grave, unknelled, uncoffined, and unknown.

His steps are not upon thy paths, – thy fields
Are not a spoil for him, – thou dost arise
And shake him from thee; the vile strength he
wields
For earth's destruction thou dost all despise,
Spurning him from thy bosom to the skies,
And sendest him, shivering in thy playful spray
And howling, to his Gods, where haply lies
His petty hope in some near port or bay,
And dashest him again to earth: – there let him
lay. . . .

And I have loved thee, Ocean! and my joy
Of youthful sports was on thy breast to be
Borne, like thy bubbles, onward: from a boy
I wantoned with thy breakers – they to me
Were a delight; and if the freshening sea
Made them a terror – 'twas a pleasing fear,
For I was as it were a child of thee,
And trusted to thy billows far and near,
And laid my hand upon thy mane – as I do here.

My task is done – my song hath ceased – my theme
Has died into an echo; it is fit
The spell should break of this protracted dream.
The torch shall be extinguished which hath lit
My midnight lamp – and what is writ, is writ, –
Would it were worthier! but I am not now
That which I have been – and my visions flit
Less palpably before me – and the glow
Which in my spirit dwelt is fluttering, faint, and low.

Farewell! a word that must be, and hath been –
A sound which makes us linger; – yet – farewell!
Ye! who have traced the Pilgrim to the scene
Which is his last, if in your memories dwell
A thought which once was his, if on ye swell
A single recollection, not in vain
He wore his sandal-shoon, and scallop-shell;
Farewell! with *him* alone may rest the pain,
If such there were – with *you*, the moral of his strain!

From THE CORSAIR

None are all evil – quickening round his heart
One softer feeling would not yet depart;
Oft could he sneer at others as beguiled
By passions worthy of a fool or child;
Yet 'gainst that passion vainly still he strove,
And even in him it asks the name of Love!
Yes, it was love – unchangeable – unchanged,
Felt but for one from whom he never ranged;
Though fairest captives daily met his eye,
He shunn'd, nor sought, but coldly pass'd them by;
Though many a beauty droop'd in prison'd bower,
None ever sooth'd his most unguarded hour.
Yes – it was Love – if thoughts of tenderness
Tried in temptation, strengthen'd by distress,
Unmoved by absence, firm in every clime,
And yet – oh more than all! untired by time;
Which nor defeated hope, nor baffled wile,
Could render sullen were she near to smile,
Nor rage could fire, nor sickness fret to vent
On her one murmur of his discontent;
Which still would meet with joy, with calmness part,
Lest that his look of grief should reach her heart;
Which nought removed, nor menaced to remove –
If there be love in mortals – this was love!
He was a villain – ay, reproaches shower
On him – but not the passion, nor its power,
Which only proved, all other virtues gone,
Not guilt itself could quench this loveliest one!

59

From LARA

There was in him a vital scorn of all:
As if the worst had fall'n which could befall,
He stood a stranger in this breathing world,
An erring spirit from another hurl'd;
A thing of dark imaginings, that shaped
By choice the perils he by chance escaped;
But 'scaped in vain, for in their memory yet
His mind would half exult and half regret:
With more capacity for love than earth
Bestows on most of mortal mould and birth,
His early dreams of good outstripp'd the truth,
And troubled manhood follow'd baffled youth;
With thought of years in phantom chase mis-spent,
And wasted powers for better purpose lent;
And fiery passions that had pour'd their wrath
In hurried desolation o'er his path,
And left the better feelings all at strife
In wild reflection o'er his stormy life;
But haughty still, and loth himself to blame,
He call'd on Nature's self to share the shame,
And charged all faults upon the fleshly form
She gave to clog the soul, and feast the worm;
Till he at last confounded good and ill,
And half mistook for fate the acts of will:
Too high for common selfishness, he could
At times resign his own for others' good,
But not in pity, not because he ought,

But in some strange perversity of thought,
That sway'd him onward with a secret pride
To do what few or none would do beside;
And this same impulse would, in tempting time,
Mislead his spirit equally to crime;
So much he soar'd beyond, or sunk beneath,
The men with whom he felt condemn'd to breathe,
And long'd by good or ill to separate
Himself from all who shared his mortal state;
His mind abhorring this, had fix'd her throne
Far from the world, in regions of her own:
Thus coldly passing all that pass'd below,
His blood in temperate seeming now would flow:
Ah! happier if it ne'er with guilt had glow'd,
But ever in that icy smoothness flow'd!
'Tis true, with other men their path he walk'd,
And like the rest in seeming did and talk'd,
Nor outraged Reason's rules by flaw nor start,
His madness was not of the head, but heart;
And rarely wander'd in his speech, or drew
His thoughts so forth as to offend the view.

EPISTLE TO AUGUSTA

My sister! my sweet sister! if a name
Dearer and purer were, it should be thine.
Mountains and seas divide us, but I claim
No tears, but tenderness to answer mine:
Go where I will, to me thou art the same –
A loved regret which I would not resign.
There yet are two things in my destiny, –
A world to roam through, and a home with thee.

The first were nothing – had I still the last,
It were the haven of my happiness;
But other claims and other ties thou hast,
And mine is not the wish to make them less.
A strange doom is thy father's son's, and past
Recalling, as it lies beyond redress;
Reversed for him our grandsire's fate of yore, –
He had no rest at sea, nor I on shore.

If my inheritance of storms hath been
In other elements, and on the rocks
Of perils, overlooked or unforeseen,
I have sustained my share of worldly shocks,
The fault was mine; nor do I seek to screen
My errors with defensive paradox;
I have been cunning in mine overthrow,
The careful pilot of my proper woe.

Mine were my faults, and mine be their reward.
My whole life was a contest, since the day
That gave me being, gave me that which marred
The gift, – a fate, or will, that walked astray;
And I at times have found the struggle hard,
And thought of shaking off my bonds of clay:
But now I fain would for a time survive,
If but to see what next can well arrive.

Kingdoms and empires in my little day
I have outlived, and yet I am not old;
And when I look on this, the petty spray
Of my own years of trouble, which have rolled
Like a wild bay of breakers, melts away:
Something – I know not what – does still uphold
A spirit of slight patience; – not in vain,
Even for its own sake, do we purchase pain.

Perhaps the workings of defiance stir
Within me – or perhaps a cold despair,
Brought on when ills habitually recur, –
Perhaps a kinder clime, or purer air,
(For even to this may change of soul refer,
And with light armour we may learn to bear,)
Have taught me a strange quiet, which was not
The chief companion of a calmer lot.

I feel almost at times as I have felt
In happy childhood; trees, and flowers, and brooks,
Which do remember me of where I dwelt
Ere my young mind was sacrificed to books,
Come as of yore upon me, and can melt
My heart with recognition of their looks;
And even at moments I could think I see
Some living things to love – but none like thee.

Here are the Alpine landscapes which create
A fund for contemplation; – to admire
Is a brief feeling of a trivial date;
But something worthier do such scenes inspire:
Here to be lonely is not desolate,
For much I view which I could most desire,
And, above all, a lake I can behold
Lovelier, not dearer, than our own of old.

Oh that thou wert but with me! – but I grow
The fool of my own wishes, and forget
The solitude which I have vaunted so
Has lost its praise in this but one regret;
There may be others which I less may show; –
I am not of the plaintive mood, and yet
I feel an ebb in my philosophy,
And the tide rising in my altered eye.

I did remind thee of our own dear Lake,
By the old Hall which may be mine no more.
Leman's is fair; but think not I forsake
The sweet remembrance of a dearer shore:
Sad havoc Time must with my memory make,
Ere *that* or *thou* can fade these eyes before;
Though, like all things which I have loved, they are
Resigned for ever, or divided far.

The world is all before me; I but ask
Of Nature that with which she will comply –
It is but in her summer's sun to bask,
To mingle with the quiet of her sky,
To see her gentle face without a mask,
And never gaze on it with apathy.
  She was my early friend, and now shall be
My sister – till I look again on thee.

I can reduce all feelings but this one;
And that I would not; – for at length I see
Such scenes as those wherein my life begun.
The earliest – even the only paths for me –
Had I but sooner learnt the crowd to shun,
I had been better than I now can be;
  The passions which have torn me would have slept;
I had not suffered, and *thou* hadst not wept.

With false Ambition what had I to do?
Little with Love, and least of all with Fame;
And yet they came unsought, and with me grew,
And made me all which they can make – a name.
Yet this was not the end I did pursue;
Surely I once beheld a nobler aim.
But all is over – I am one the more
To baffled millions which have gone before.

And for the future, this world's future may
From me demand but little of my care;
I have outlived myself by many a day;
Having survived so many things that were;
My years have been no slumber, but the prey
Of ceaseless vigils; for I had the share
Of life which might have filled a century,
Before its fourth in time had passed me by.

And for the remnant which may be to come
I am content; and for the past I feel
Not thankless, – for within the crowded sum
Of struggles, happiness at times would steal,
And for the present, I would not benumb
My feelings farther. – Nor shall I conceal
That with all this I still can look around,
And worship Nature with a thought profound.

For thee, my own sweet sister, in thy heart
I know myself secure, as thou in mine;
We were and are – I am, even as thou art –
Beings who ne'er each other can resign;
It is the same, together or apart,
From life's commencement to its slow decline
We are entwined – let death come slow or fast,
The tie which bound the first endures the last!

LINES ON HEARING THAT LADY BYRON WAS ILL

And thou wert sad – yet I was not with thee;
    And thou wert sick, and yet I was not near;
Methought that joy and health alone could be
    Where I was *not* – and pain and sorrow here!
And is it thus? – it is as I foretold,
    And shall be more so; for the mind recoils
Upon itself, and the wrecked heart lies cold,
    While heaviness collects the shattered spoils.
It is not in the storm nor in the strife
    We feel benumbed, and wish to be no more,
    But in the after-silence on the shore,
When all is lost, except a little life.

I am too well avenged! – but 'twas my right;
    Whate'er my sins might be, *thou* wert not sent
To be the Nemesis who should requite –
    Nor did Heaven choose so near an instrument.
Mercy is for the merciful! – if thou
Hast been of such, 'twill be accorded now.
Thy nights are banished from the realms of sleep. –
    Yes! they may flatter thee, but thou shalt feel
    A hollow agony which will not heal,
For thou art pillowed on a course too deep;
Thou hast sown in my sorrow, and must reap
    The bitter harvest in a woe as real!
I have had many foes, but none like thee;
    For 'gainst the rest myself I could defend,

And be avenged, or turn them into friend;
But thou in safe implacability
Hadst nought to dread – in thy own weakness shielded,
And in my love, which hath but too much yielded,
    And spared, for thy sake, some I should not spare;
And thus upon the world – trust in thy truth,
And the wild fame of my ungoverned youth –
    On things that were not, and on things that are –
Even upon such a basis hast thou built
A monument, whose cement hath been guilt!
    The moral Clytemnestra of thy lord,
    And hewed down, with an unsuspected sword,
Fame, peace, and hope – and all the better life
    Which, but for this cold treason of thy heart,
Might still have risen from out the grave of strife,
    And found a nobler duty than to part.
But of thy virtues didst thou make a vice,
    Trafficking with them in a purpose cold,
    For present anger, and for future gold –
And buying other's grief at any price.
And thus once entered into crooked ways,
The early truth, which was thy proper praise,
Did not still walk beside thee – but at times,
And with a breast unknowing its own crimes,
Deceit, averments incompatible,
Equivocations, and the thoughts which dwell
    In Janus-spirits – the significant eye
Which learns to lie with silence – the pretext
Of prudence, with advantages annexed –

The acquiescence in all things which tend,
No matter how, to the desired end –
    All found a place in thy philosophy.
The means were worthy, and the end is won –
I would not do by thee as thou hast done!

From BEPPO

They've pretty faces yet, those same Venetians,
  Black eyes, arched brows, and sweet expressions still;
Such as of old were copied from the Grecians,
  In ancient arts by moderns mimicked ill;
And like so many Venuses of Titian's
  (The best's at Florence – see it, if ye will,)
They look when leaning over the balcony,
Or stepped from out a picture by Giorgione,

Whose tints are truth and beauty at their best;
  And when you to Manfrini's palace go,
That picture (howsoever fine the rest)
  Is loveliest to my mind of all the show;
It may perhaps be also to *your* zest,
  And that's the cause I rhyme upon it so:
'Tis but a portrait of his son, and wife,
And self; but *such* a woman! love in life!

Love in full life and length, not love ideal,
    No, nor ideal beauty, that fine name,
But something better still, so very real,
    That the sweet model must have been the same;
A thing that you would purchase, beg, or steal,
    Wer't not impossible, besides a shame:
The face recalls some face, as 'twere with pain,
You once have seen, but ne'er will see again;

One of those forms which flit by us, when we
    Are young, and fix our eyes on every face;
And, oh! the loveliness at times we see
    In momentary gliding, the soft grace,
The youth, the bloom, the beauty which agree,
    In many a nameless being we retrace,
Whose course and home we knew not, nor shall know,
Like the lost Pleiad seen no more below.

I said that like a picture by Giorgione
   Venetian women were, and so they *are*,
Particularly seen from a balcony,
   (For beauty's sometimes best set off afar)
And there, just like a heroine of Goldoni,
   They peep from out the blind, or o'er the bar;
And truth to say, they're mostly very pretty,
And rather like to show it, more's the pity!

For glances beget ogles, ogles sighs,
   Sighs wishes, wishes words, and words a letter,
Which flies on wings of light-heeled Mercuries,
   Who do such things because they know no better;
And then, God knows what mischief may arise,
   When love links two young people in one fetter,
Vile assignations, and adulterous beds,
Elopements, broken vows, and hearts, and heads.

Shakespeare described the sex in Desdemona
  As very fair, but yet suspect in fame,
And to this day from Venice to Verona
  Such matters may be probably the same,
Except that since those times was never known a
  Husband whom mere suspicion could inflame
To suffocate a wife no more than twenty,
Because she had a 'cavalier servente.'

Their jealousy (if they are ever jealous)
  Is of a fair complexion altogether,
Not like that sooty devil of Othello's,
  Which smothers women in a bed of feather,
But worthier of these much more jolly fellows,
  When weary of the matrimonial tether
His head for such a wife no mortal bothers,
But takes at once another, or another's.

Didst ever see a Gondola? For fear
   You should not, I'll describe it you exactly:
'Tis a long covered boat that's common here,
   Carved at the prow, built lightly, but compactly,
Rowed by two rowers, each called 'Gondolier,'
   It glides along the water looking blackly,
Just like a coffin clapt in a canoe,
Where none can make out what you say or do.

And up and down the long canals they go,
   And under the Rialto shoot along,
By night and day, all paces, swift or slow,
   And round the theatres, a sable throng,
They wait in their dusk livery of woe –
   But not to them do woeful things belong,
For sometimes they contain a deal of fun,
Like mourning coaches when the funeral's done.

DON JUAN

From Canto 1

'They tell me 'tis decided; you depart.
　'Tis wise, 'tis well, but not the less a pain.
I have no further claim on your young heart;
　Mine was the victim and would be again.
To love too much has been the only art
　I used. I write in haste, and if a stain
Be on this sheet, 'tis not what it appears;
My eyeballs burn and throb, but have no tears.

'I loved, I love you, for that love have lost
　State, station, heaven, mankind's, my own esteem,
And yet cannot regret what it hath cost,
　So dear is still the memory of that dream.
Yet if I name my guilt, 'tis not to boast;
　None can deem harshlier of me than I deem.
I trace this scrawl because I cannot rest.
I've nothing to reproach or to request.

'Man's love is of his life a thing apart,
    'Tis woman's whole existence. Man may range
The court, camp, church, the vessel, and the mart;
    Sword, gown, gain, glory offer in exchange
Pride, fame, ambition to fill up his heart,
    And few there are whom these cannot estrange.
Man has all these resources, we but one,
To mourn alone the love which has undone.

'You will proceed in beauty and in pride,
    Beloved and loving many. All is o'er
For me on earth, except some years to hide
    My shame and sorrow deep in my heart's core.
These I could bear, but cannot cast aside
    The passion which still rends it as before.
And so farewell – forgive me, love me – no,
That word is idle now, but let it go.

'My breast has been all weakness, is so yet;
    I struggle, but cannot collect my mind.
My blood still rushes where my spirit's set,
    As roll the waves before the settled wind.
My brain is feminine nor can forget;
    To all, except your image, madly blind.
As turns the needle trembling to the pole
It ne'er can reach, so turns to you my soul.

'I have no more to say, but linger still
    And dare not set my seal upon this sheet,
And yet I may as well the task fulfil,
    My misery can scarce be more complete.
I had not lived till now, could sorrow kill;
    Death flies the wretch who fain the blow would
    meet,
And I must even survive this last adieu
And bear with life, to love and pray for you.'

DON JUAN

From Canto 1

No more – no more – oh never more on me
   The freshness of the heart can fall like dew,
Which out of all the lovely things we see
   Extracts emotions beautiful and new,
Hived in our bosoms like the bag o' the bee.
   Think'st thou the honey with those objects grew?
Alas, 'twas not in them, but in thy power
To double even the sweetness of a flower.

No more – no more – oh never more, my heart,
   Canst thou be my sole world, my universe!
Once all in all, but now a thing apart,
   Thou canst not be my blessing or my curse.
The illusion's gone forever, and thou art
   Insensible, I trust, but none the worse,
And in thy stead I've got a deal of judgement,
Though heaven knows how it ever found a lodgement.

My days of love are over, me no more
    The charms of maid, wife, and still less of widow
Can make the fool of which they made before;
    In short, I must not lead the life I did do.
The credulous hope of mutual minds is o'er,
    The copious use of claret is forbid too,
So for a good old-gentlemanly vice,
I think I must take up with avarice.

Ambition was my idol, which was broken
    Before the shrines of Sorrow and of Pleasure;
And the two last have left me many a token
    O'er which reflection may be made at leisure.
Now, like Friar Bacon's brazen head, I've spoken,
    'Time is, Time was, Time's past.' A chymic treasure
Is glittering youth, which I have spent betimes,
My heart in passion and my head on rhymes.

What is the end of fame? 'Tis but to fill
    A certain portion of uncertain paper.
Some liken it to climbing up a hill,
    Whose summit, like all hills, is lost in vapour.
For this men write, speak, preach, and heroes kill,
    And bards burn what they call their midnight taper,
To have, when the original is dust,
A name, a wretched picture, and worse bust.

What are the hopes of man? Old Egypt's King
    Cheops erected the first pyramid,
And largest, thinking it was just the thing
    To keep his memory whole and mummy hid;
But somebody or other rummaging,
    Burglariously broke his coffin's lid.
Let not a monument give you or me hopes,
Since not a pinch of dust remains of Cheops.

But I being fond of true philosophy
    Say very often to myself, 'Alas!
All things that have been born were born to die,
    And flesh (which Death mows down to hay) is
      grass.
You've passed your youth not so unpleasantly,
    And if you had it o'er again, 'twould pass;
So thank your stars that matters are no worse
And read your Bible, sir, and mind your purse.'

But for the present, gentle reader, and
    Still gentler purchaser, the bard – that's I –
Must with permission shake you by the hand,
    And so your humble servant, and good-bye.
We meet again, if we should understand
    Each other; and if not, I shall not try
Your patience further than by this short sample.
'Twere well if others followed my example.

'Go, little book, from this my solitude!
   I cast thee on the waters, go thy ways!
And if, as I believe, thy vein be good,
   The world will find thee after many days.'
When Southey's read, and Wordsworth understood,
   I can't help putting in my claim to praise.
The four first rhymes are Southey's every line;
For God's sake, reader, take them not for mine.

DON JUAN

From Canto 2

It was the cooling hour, just when the rounded
    Red sun sinks down behind the azure hill,
Which then seems as if the whole earth it bounded,
    Circling all nature, hushed and dim and still,
With the far mountain-crescent half surrounded
    On one side, and the deep sea calm and chill
Upon the other, and the rosy sky
With one star sparkling through it like an eye.

And thus they wandered forth, and hand in hand,
    Over the shining pebbles and the shells,
Glided along the smooth and hardened sand,
    And in the worn and wild receptacles
Worked by the storms, yet worked as it were planned,
    In hollow halls with sparry roofs and cells,
They turned to rest, and each clasped by an arm,
Yielded to the deep twilight's purple charm.

They looked up to the sky, whose floating glow
   Spread like a rosy ocean, vast and bright.
They gazed upon the glittering sea below,
   Whence the broad moon rose circling into sight.
They heard the wave's splash and the wind so low,
   And saw each other's dark eyes darting light
Into each other, and beholding this,
Their lips drew near and clung into a kiss,

A long, long kiss, a kiss of youth and love
   And beauty, all concentrating like rays
Into one focus, kindled from above;
   Such kisses as belong to early days,
Where heart and soul and sense in concert move,
   And the blood's lava, and the pulse a blaze,
Each kiss a heart-quake, for a kiss's strength,
I think, it must be reckoned by its length.

By length I mean duration; theirs endured
   Heaven knows how long; no doubt they never
   reckoned,
And if they had, they could not have secured
   The sum of their sensations to a second.
They had not spoken, but they felt allured,
   As if their souls and lips each other beckoned,
Which, being joined, like swarming bees they clung,
Their hearts the flowers from whence the honey
   sprung.

They were alone, but not alone as they
   Who shut in chambers think it loneliness.
The silent ocean and the starlight bay,
   The twilight glow, which momently grew less,
The voiceless sands and dropping caves, that lay
   Around them, made them to each other press,
As if there were no life beneath the sky
Save theirs, and that their life could never die.

They feared no eyes nor ears on that lone beach,
  They felt no terrors from the night, they were
All in all to each other. Though their speech
  Was broken words, they thought a language there,
And all the burning tongues the passions teach
  Found in one sigh the best interpreter
Of nature's oracle, first love, that all
Which Eve has left her daughters since her fall.

Haidée spoke not of scruples, asked no vows
  Nor offered any; she had never heard
Of plight and promises to be a spouse,
  Or perils by a loving maid incurred.
She was all which pure ignorance allows
  And flew to her young mate like a young bird,
And never having dreamt of falsehood, she
Had not one word to say of constancy.

She loved and was belovèd, she adored
   And she was worshipped after nature's fashion.
Their intense souls, into each other poured,
   If souls could die, had perished in that passion,
But by degrees their senses were restored,
   Again to be o'ercome, again to dash on.
And beating 'gainst *his* bosom, Haidée's heart
Felt as if never more to beat apart.

Alas, they were so young, so beautiful,
   So lonely, loving, helpless, and the hour
Was that in which the heart is always full,
   And having o'er itself no further power,
Prompts deeds eternity cannot annul,
   But pays off moments in an endless shower
Of hell-fire, all prepared for people giving
   Pleasure or pain to one another living.

Alas for Juan and Haidée! They were
    So loving and so lovely; till then never,
Excepting our first parents, such a pair
    Had run the risk of being damned forever.
And Haidée, being devout as well as fair,
    Had doubtless heard about the Stygian river
And hell and purgatory, but forgot
Just in the very crisis she should not.

They look upon each other, and their eyes
    Gleam in the moonlight, and her white arm clasps
Round Juan's head, and his around hers lies
    Half buried in the tresses which it grasps.
She sits upon his knee and drinks his sighs,
    He hers, until they end in broken gasps;
And thus they form a group that's quite antique,
Half naked, loving, natural, and Greek.

And when those deep and burning moments passed,
    And Juan sunk to sleep within her arms,
She slept not, but all tenderly, though fast,
    Sustained his head upon her bosom's charms.
And now and then her eye to heaven is cast,
    And then on the pale cheek her breast now warms,
Pillowed on her o'erflowing heart, which pants
With all it granted and with all it grants.

An infant when it gazes on a light,
    A child the moment when it drains the breast,
A devotee when soars the Host in sight,
    An Arab with a stranger for a guest,
A sailor when the prize has struck in fight,
    A miser filling his most hoarded chest
Feel rapture, but not such true joy are reaping
As they who watch o'er what they love while sleeping.

For there it lies so tranquil, so beloved;
   All that it hath of life with us is living,
So gentle, stirless, helpless, and unmoved,
   And all unconscious of the joy 'tis giving.
All it hath felt, inflicted, passed, and proved,
   Hushed into depths beyond the watcher's diving,
There lies the thing we love with all its errors
And all its charms, like death without its terrors.

The lady watched her lover; and that hour
   Of love's and night's and ocean's solitude
O'erflowed her soul with their united power.
   Amidst the barren sand and rocks so rude
She and her wave-worn love had made their bower,
   Where nought upon their passion could intrude,
And all the stars that crowded the blue space
Saw nothing happier than her glowing face.

Alas, the love of women! It is known
    To be a lovely and a fearful thing,
For all of theirs upon that die is thrown,
    And if 'tis lost, life hath no more to bring
To them but mockeries of the past alone,
    And their revenge is as the tiger's spring,
Deadly and quick and crushing; yet as real
Torture is theirs, what they inflict they feel.

They are right, for man, to man so oft unjust,
    Is always so to women. One sole bond
Awaits them, treachery is all their trust.
    Taught to conceal, their bursting hearts despond
Over their idol, till some wealthier lust
    Buys them in marriage – and what rests beyond?
A thankless husband, next a faithless lover,
Then dressing, nursing, praying, and all's over.

Some take a lover, some take drams or prayers,
  Some mind their household, others dissipation,
Some run away and but exchange their cares,
  Losing the advantage of a virtuous station.
Few changes e'er can better their affairs,
  Theirs being an unnatural situation,
From the dull palace to the dirty hovel.
Some play the devil, and then write a novel.

Haidée was Nature's bride and knew not this;
  Haidée was Passion's child, born where the sun
Showers triple light and scorches even the kiss
  Of his gazelle-eyed daughters. She was one
Made but to love, to feel that she was his
  Who was her chosen. What was said or done
Elsewhere was nothing. She had nought to fear,
Hope, care, nor love beyond; her heart beat here.

DON JUAN

From Canto 3

Oh love, what is it in this world of ours
  Which makes it fatal to be loved? Ah why
With cypress branches hast thou wreathed thy bowers
  And made thy best interpreter a sigh?
As those who dote on odours pluck the flowers
  And place them on their breast – but place to die;
Thus the frail beings we would fondly cherish
Are laid within our bosoms but to perish.

In her first passion woman loves her lover,
  In all the others all she loves is love,
Which grows a habit she can ne'er get over
  And fits her loosely like an easy glove,
As you may find whene'er you like to prove her.
  One man alone at first her heart can move;
She then prefers him in the plural number,
Not finding that the additions much encumber.

I know not if the fault be men's or theirs,
    But one thing's pretty sure: a woman planted
(Unless at once she plunge for life in prayers)
    After a decent time must be gallanted,
Although no doubt her first of love affairs
    Is that to which her heart is wholly granted.
Yet there are some, they say, who have had none,
But those who have ne'er end with only one.

'Tis melancholy and a fearful sign
    Of human frailty, folly, also crime,
That love and marriage rarely can combine,
    Although they both are born in the same clime.
Marriage from love, like vinegar from wine –
    A sad, sour, sober beverage – by time
Is sharpened from its high celestial flavour
Down to a very homely household savour.

There's something of antipathy, as 'twere,
    Between their present and their future state.
A kind of flattery that's hardly fair
    Is used until the truth arrives too late.
Yet what can people do, except despair?
    The same things change their names at such a rate;
For instance, passion in a lover's glorious,
But in a husband is pronounced uxorious.

Men grow ashamed of being so very fond;
 They sometimes also get a little tired
(But that, of course, is rare) and then despond.
 The same things cannot always be admired,
Yet 'tis 'so nominated in the bond'
 That both are tied till one shall have expired.
Sad thought! to lose the spouse that was adorning
Our days, and put one's servants into mourning.

There's doubtless something in domestic doings,
 Which forms in fact true love's antithesis.
Romances paint at full length people's wooings,
 But only give a bust of marriages,
For no one cares for matrimonial cooings;
 There's nothing wrong in a connubial kiss.
Think you, if Laura had been Petrarch's wife,
He would have written sonnets all his life?

From DON JUAN

The isles of Greece, the isles of Greece!
   Where burning Sappho loved and sung,
Where grew the arts of war and peace,
   Where Delos rose, and Phoebus sprung,
Eternal summer gilds them yet,
But all, except their sun, is set.

The Scian and the Teian Muse,
   The hero's harp, the lover's lute
Have found the fame your shores refuse.
   Their place of birth alone is mute
To sounds which echo further west
Than your sires' 'Islands of the Blest'.

The mountains look on Marathon,
   And Marathon looks on the sea.
And musing there an hour alone,
   I dreamed that Greece might still be free,
For standing on the Persian's grave,
I could not deem myself a slave.

A king sate on the rocky brow
   Which looks o'er sea-born Salamis;
And ships by thousands lay below,
   And men in nations – all were his!
He counted them at break of day,
And when the sun set where were they?

And where are they? And where art thou,
   My country? On thy voiceless shore
The heroic lay is tuneless now,
   The heroic bosom beats no more!
And must thy lyre, so long divine,
Degenerate into hands like mine?

'Tis something in the dearth of fame,
   Though linked among a fettered race,
To feel at least a patriot's shame,
   Even as I sing, suffuse my face.
For what is left the poet here?
For Greeks a blush, for Greece a tear.

Must we but weep o'er days more blest?
   Must we but blush? Our fathers bled.
Earth! Render back from out thy breast
   A remnant of our Spartan dead!
Of the three hundred grant but three,
To make a new Thermopylae!

What, silent still? And silent all?
   Ah no! The voices of the dead
Sound like a distant torrent's fall
   And answer, 'Let one living head,
But one arise – we come, we come!'
'Tis but the living who are dumb.

In vain – in vain – strike other chords.
   Fill high the cup with Samian wine!
Leave battles to the Turkish hordes,
   And shed the blood of Scio's vine!
Hark, rising to the ignoble call,
How answers each bold bacchanal!

You have the Pyrrhic dance as yet,
  Where is the Pyrrhic phalanx gone?
Of two such lessons, why forget
  The nobler and the manlier one?
You have the letters Cadmus gave;
Think ye he meant them for a slave?

Fill high the bowl with Samian wine!
  We will not think of themes like these.
It made Anacreon's song divine;
  He served, but served Polycrates,
A tyrant; but our masters then
Were still at least our countrymen.

The tyrant of the Chersonese
  Was freedom's best and bravest friend.
That tyrant was Miltiades.
  Oh that the present hour would lend
Another despot of the kind!
Such chains as his were sure to bind.

Fill high the bowl with Samian wine!
    On Suli's rock and Parga's shore,
Exists the remnant of a line
    Such as the Doric mothers bore.
And there perhaps some seed is sown,
The Heracleidan blood might own.

Trust not for freedom to the Franks;
    They have a king who buys and sells.
In native swords and native ranks
    The only hope of courage dwells,
But Turkish force and Latin fraud
Would break your shield, however broad.

Fill high the bowl with Samian wine!
    Our virgins dance beneath the shade.
I see their glorious black eyes shine,
    But gazing on each glowing maid,
My own the burning teardrop laves,
To think such breasts must suckle slaves.

Place me on Sunium's marbled steep,
　　Where nothing, save the waves and I,
May hear our mutual murmurs sweep;
　　There, swan-like, let me sing and die.
A land of slaves shall ne'er be mine –
Dash down yon cup of Samian wine!

DON JUAN

From Canto 4

Their faces were not made for wrinkles, their
  Pure blood to stagnate, their great hearts to fail.
The blank grey was not made to blast their hair,
  But like the climes that know nor snow nor hail
They were all summer. Lightning might assail
  And shiver them to ashes, but to trail
A long and snake-like life of dull decay
Was not for them – they had too little clay.

They were alone once more; for them to be
  Thus was another Eden. They were never
Weary, unless when separate. The tree
  Cut from its forest root of years, the river
Dammed from its fountain, the child from the knee
  And breast maternal weaned at once forever
Would wither less than these two torn apart.
Alas, there is no instinct like the heart –

The heart – which may be broken. Happy they,
   Thrice fortunate who of that fragile mould,
The precious porcelain of human clay,
   Break with the first fall. They can ne'er behold
The long year linked with heavy day on day
   And all which must be borne and never told,
While life's strange principle will often lie
Deepest in those who long the most to die.

'Whom the gods love die young' was said of yore,
   And many deaths do they escape by this:
The death of friends and that which slays even more,
   The death of friendship, love, youth, all that is,
Except mere breath. And since the silent shore
   Awaits at last even those whom longest miss
The old archer's shafts, perhaps the early grave,
Which men weep over, may be meant to save.

Haidée and Juan thought not of the dead.
  The heavens and earth and air seemed made for
  them.
They found no fault with Time, save that he fled.
  They saw not in themselves aught to condemn;
Each was the other's mirror, and but read
  Joy sparkling in their dark eyes like a gem,
And knew such brightness was but the reflection
Of their exchanging glances of affection.

The gentle pressure and the thrilling touch,
  The least glance better understood than words,
Which still said all and ne'er could say too much,
  A language too, but like to that of birds,
Known but to them, at least appearing such
  As but to lovers a true sense affords,
Sweet playful phrases, which would seem absurd
To those who have ceased to hear such, or ne'er
  heard.

All these were theirs, for they were children still
   And children still they should have ever been.
They were not made in the real world to fill
   A busy character in the dull scene,
But like two beings born from out a rill,
   A nymph and her belovèd, all unseen
To pass their lives in fountains and on flowers
And never know the weight of human hours.

Moons changing had rolled on, and changeless found
   Those their bright rise had lighted to such joys
As rarely they beheld throughout their round.
   And these were not of the vain kind which cloys,
For theirs were buoyant spirits, never bound
   By the mere senses. And that which destroys
Most love, possession, unto them appeared
A thing which each endearment more endeared.

Oh beautiful and rare as beautiful!
  But theirs was love in which the mind delights
To lose itself, when the old world grows dull
  And we are sick of its hack sounds and sights,
Intrigues, adventures of the common school,
  Its petty passions, marriages, and flights,
Where Hymen's torch but brands one strumpet more,
Whose husband only knows her not a whore.

Hard words, harsh truth – a truth which many know.
  Enough. The faithful and the fairy pair,
Who never found a single hour too slow,
  What was it made them thus exempt from care?
Young innate feelings all have felt below,
  Which perish in the rest, but in them were
Inherent; what we mortals call romantic
And always envy, though we deem it frantic.

This is in others a factitious state,
   An opium dream of too much youth and reading,
But was in them their nature or their fate.
   No novels e'er had set their young hearts bleeding,
For Haidée's knowledge was by no means great,
   And Juan was a boy of saintly breeding,
So that there was no reason for their loves
More than for those of nightingales or doves.

They gazed upon the sunset; 'tis an hour
   Dear unto all, but dearest to *their* eyes,
For it had made them what they were. The power
   Of love had first o'erwhelmed them from such skies,
When happiness had been their only dower,
   And twilight saw them linked in passion's ties.
Charmed with each other, all things charmed that
   brought
The past still welcome as the present thought.

I know not why, but in that hour tonight
  Even as they gazed, a sudden tremor came
And swept, as 'twere, across their heart's delight,
  Like the wind o'er a harpstring or a flame,
When one is shook in sound, and one in sight;
  And thus some boding flashed through either frame
And called from Juan's breast a faint low sigh,
While one new tear arose in Haidée's eye.

That large black prophet eye seemed to dilate
  And follow far the disappearing sun,
As if their last day of a happy date
  With his broad, bright, and dropping orb were
    gone.
Juan gazed on her as to ask his fate;
  He felt a grief, but knowing cause for none,
His glance inquired of hers for some excuse
For feelings causeless, or at least abstruse.

She turned to him and smiled, but in that sort
    Which makes not others smile, then turned aside.
Whatever feeling shook her, it seemed short
    And mastered by her wisdom or her pride.
When Juan spoke too – it might be in sport –
    Of this their mutual feeling, she replied,
'If it should be so, but – it cannot be –
Or I at least shall not survive to see.'

Juan would question further, but she pressed
    His lip to hers and silenced him with this,
And then dismissed the omen from her breast,
    Defying augury with that fond kiss.
And no doubt of all methods 'tis the best;
    Some people prefer wine – 'tis not amiss.
I have tried both; so those who would a part take
May choose between the headache and the heartache.

One of the two, according to your choice,
   Woman or wine, you'll have to undergo.
Both maladies are taxes on our joys;
   But which to choose, I really hardly know,
And if I had to give a casting voice,
   For both sides I could many reasons show,
And then decide, without great wrong to either,
It were much better to have both than neither.

Juan and Haidée gazed upon each other
   With swimming looks of speechless tenderness,
Which mixed all feelings, friend, child, lover, brother,
   All that the best can mingle and express
When two pure hearts are poured in one another
   And love too much and yet cannot love less,
But almost sanctify the sweet excess
By the immortal wish and power to bless.

Mixed in each other's arms and heart in heart,
    Why did they not then die? They had lived too long
Should an hour come to bid them breathe apart.
    Years could but bring them cruel things or wrong;
The world was not for them, nor the world's art
    For beings passionate as Sappho's song.
Love was born *with* them, *in* them, so intense,
It was their very spirit – not a sense.

They should have lived together deep in woods,
    Unseen as sings the nightingale. They were
Unfit to mix in these thick solitudes
    Called social, haunts of hate and vice and care.
How lonely every freeborn creature broods!
    The sweetest songbirds nestle in a pair;
The eagle soars alone; the gull and crow
Flock o'er their carrion, just like men below.

Now pillowed cheek to cheek in loving sleep,
    Haidée and Juan their siesta took,
A gentle slumber, but it was not deep,
    For ever and anon a something shook
Juan and shuddering o'er his frame would creep;
    And Haidée's sweet lips murmured like a brook
A wordless music, and her face so fair
Stirred with her dream as rose leaves with the air.

Or as the stirring of a deep clear stream
    Within an Alpine hollow when the wind
Walks o'er it, was she shaken by the dream,
    The mystical usurper of the mind,
O'erpowering us to be whate'er may seem
    Good to the soul which we no more can bind.
Strange state of being (for 'tis still to be),
Senseless to feel and with sealed eyes to see!

She dreamed of being alone on the seashore,
    Chained to a rock. She knew not how, but stir
She could not from the spot, and the loud roar
    Grew, and each wave rose roughly, threatening her,
And o'er her upper lip they seemed to pour,
    Until she sobbed for breath, and soon they were
Foaming o'er her lone head, so fierce and high
Each broke to drown her, yet she could not die.

Anon she was released, and then she strayed
    O'er the sharp shingles with her bleeding feet,
And stumbled almost every step she made.
    And something rolled before her in a sheet,
Which she must still pursue howe'er afraid.
    'Twas white and indistinct, nor stopped to meet
Her glance nor grasp, for still she gazed and grasped
And ran, but it escaped her as she clasped.

The dream changed. In a cave she stood, its walls
  Were hung with marble icicles, the work
Of ages on its water-fretted halls,
  Where waves might wash, and seals might breed
  and lurk.
Her hair was dripping, and the very balls
  Of her black eyes seemed turned to tears, and murk
The sharp rocks looked below each drop they caught,
Which froze to marble as it fell, she thought.

And wet and cold and lifeless at her feet,
  Pale as the foam that frothed on his dead brow,
Which she essayed in vain to clear (how sweet
  Were once her cares, how idle seemed they now),
Lay Juan, nor could aught renew the beat
  Of his quenched heart. And the sea dirges low
Rang in her sad ears like a mermaid's song,
And that brief dream appeared a life too long.

DON JUAN

From Canto 11

Juan knew several languages, as well
    He might, and brought them up with skill in time
To save his fame with each accomplished belle,
    Who still regretted that he did not rhyme.
There wanted but this requisite to swell
    His qualities (with them) into sublime.
Lady Fitz-Frisky and Miss Maevia Mannish
Both longed extremely to be sung in Spanish.

However, he did pretty well and was
    Admitted as an aspirant to all
The coteries, and as in Banquo's glass,
    At great assemblies or in parties small
He saw ten thousand living authors pass,
    That being about their average numeral;
Also the eighty 'greatest living poets',
As every paltry magazine can show *it's*.

In twice five years the 'greatest living poet',
    Like to the champion in the fisty ring,
Is called on to support his claim or show it,
    Although 'tis an imaginary thing.
Even I, albeit I'm sure I did not know it
    Nor sought of foolscap subjects to be king,
Was reckoned a considerable time
The grand Napoleon of the realms of rhyme.

But Juan was my Moscow, and Faliero
    My Leipsic, and my Mont Saint Jean seems Cain.
'La Belle Alliance' of dunces down at zero,
    Now that the lion's fallen, may rise again.
But I will fall at least as fell my hero,
    Nor reign at all, or as a monarch reign,
Or to some lonely isle of jailors go
With turncoat Southey for my turnkey Lowe.

Sir Walter reigned before me, Moore and Campbell
  Before and after; but now grown more holy,
The Muses upon Sion's hill must ramble
  With poets almost clergymen, or wholly,
And Pegasus hath a psalmodic amble
  Beneath the very Reverend Rowley Powley,
Who shoes the glorious animal with stilts,
A modern Ancient Pistol – by the hilts!

Still he excels that artificial hard
  Labourer in the same vineyard – though the vine
Yields him but vinegar for his reward –
  That neutralized dull Dorus of the Nine,
That swarthy Sporus, neither man nor bard,
  That ox of verse, who ploughs for every line.
Cambyses' roaring Romans beat at least
The howling Hebrews of Cybele's priest.

Then there's my gentle Euphues, who, they say,
  Sets up for being a sort of moral me.
He'll find it rather difficult some day
  To turn out both, or either, it may be.
Some persons think that Coleridge hath the sway,
  And Wordsworth has supporters, two or three,
And that deep-mouthed Boeotian, Savage Landor,
Has taken for a swan rogue Southey's gander.

John Keats, who was killed off by one critique,
  Just as he really promised something great,
If not intelligible, without Greek
  Contrived to talk about the gods of late,
Much as they might have been supposed to speak.
  Poor fellow! His was an untoward fate.
'Tis strange the mind, that very fiery particle,
Should let itself be snuffed out by an article.

The list grows long of live and dead pretenders
    To that which none will gain; or none will know
The conqueror at least, who, ere Time renders
    His last award, will have the long grass grow
Above his burnt-out brain and sapless cinders.
    If I might augur, I should rate but low
Their chances; they're too numerous, like the thirty
Mock tyrants when Rome's annals waxed but dirty.

This is the literary lower empire,
    Where the Praetorian bands take up the matter,
A 'dreadful trade' like his who 'gathers samphire',
    The insolent soldiery to soothe and flatter
With the same feelings as you'd coax a vampire.
    Now were I once at home and in good satire,
I'd try conclusions with those Janizaries
And show them what an intellectual war is.

I think I know a trick or two would turn
    Their flanks, but it is hardly worth my while
With such small gear to give myself concern.
    Indeed I've not the necessary bile;
My natural temper's really aught but stern,
    And even my Muse's worst reproof's a smile,
And then she drops a brief and modern curtsy
And glides away, assured she never hurts ye.

STANZAS

Written on the road between Florence and Pisa

Oh, talk not to me of a name great in story;
The days of your youth are the days of our glory;
And the myrtle and ivy of sweet two-and-twenty
Are worth all your laurels, though ever so plenty.

What are garlands and crowns to the brow that is
   wrinkled?
'Tis but as a dead-flower with May-dew besprinkled.
Then away with all such from the head that is hoary!
What care I for the wreaths that can *only* give glory?

Oh Fame! – if I e'er took delight in thy praises,
'Twas less for the sake of thy high-sounding phrases,
Than to see the bright eyes of the dear one discover
She thought that I was not unworthy to love her.

There chiefly I sought thee, *there* only I found thee;
Her glance was the best of the rays that surround
   thee;
When it sparkled o'er aught that was bright in my
   story,
I knew it was love, and I felt it was glory.

ON THIS DAY I COMPLETE MY THIRTY-SIXTH YEAR

'Tis time this heart should be unmoved,
   Since others it hath ceased to move:
Yet, though I cannot be beloved,
      Still let me love!

My days are in the yellow leaf;
   The flowers and fruits of love are gone;
The worm, the canker, and the grief
      Are mine alone!

The fire that on my bosom preys
   Is lone as some volcanic isle;
No torch is kindled at its blaze –
      A funeral pile.

The hope, the fear, the jealous care,
   The exalted portion of the pain
And power of love, I cannot share,
      But wear the chain.

But 'tis not *thus* – and 'tis not *here* –
   Such thoughts should shake my soul, nor *now*,
Where glory decks the hero's bier,
      Or binds his brow.

The sword, the banner, and the field,
  Glory and Greece, around me see!
The Spartan, borne upon his shield,
      Was not more free.

Awake! (not Greece – she *is* awake!)
  Awake, my spirit! Think through *whom*
Thy life-blood tracks its parent lake,
      And then strike home!

Tread those reviving passions down,
  Unworthy manhood! – unto thee
Indifferent should the smile or frown
      Of beauty be.

If thou regret'st thy youth, *why live?*
  The land of honourable death
Is here: – up to the field, and give
      Away thy breath!

Seek out – less often sought than found –
  A soldier's grave, for thee the best;
Then look around, and choose thy ground,
      And take thy rest.